Brian Dembowczyk

CORNERSTONES

200

Questions & Answers to Learn Truth

B&H
KIDS
Nashville, Tennessee

Dedication

To Landry Holmes, Jeremy Carroll, Alyssa Jones, Rachel Myrick, Karen Jones, Sam O'Neil, and Keith Tyrrell. Thank you for investing so abundantly, passionately, and joyfully to position kids ministry leaders and parents around the world to teach children theology and to help them encounter the beauty of the gospel and love Jesus Christ.

Copyright © 2018 by Brian Dembowczyk
All rights reserved. 978-1-4627-8234-5
Published by B&H Publishing Group, Nashville, Tennessee
All Scripture quotations are taken from the Christian
Standard Bible®, Copyright © 2017 by Holman Bible Publishers.
Used by permission. Christian Standard Bible® and CSB® are
federally registered trademarks of Holman Bible Publishers.
DEWEY: 230   SUBHD: CHRISTIANITY—DOCTRINES / CHRISTIAN LIFE
Illustrations by Kristi Smith and Diana Lawrence
Printed in Shenzhen, Guangdong, China in December 2017
1 2 3 4 5 6 · 22 21 20 19 18

Dear parent,

Recently, some families in our church gathered for a game of kickball. We threw four bases down in the grass, chose teams, and began to play. When it was my turn to kick, I booted the ball and ran, watching the play unfold before me. I rounded first and continued to run as I watched the opposing team field the ball. A few seconds later, I glanced down to step onto second base. But it wasn't there. Confused, I looked around and realized it was about fifteen feet to my left. I had run in the wrong direction! I scampered to the bag, relieved the opposing team had tried to make a play elsewhere.

That base-running blunder helps me understand God's heart behind one of the classic Scriptures on parenting: "Start a youth out on his way; even when he grows old he will not depart from it" (Proverbs 22:6).

I'm far from a youth these days, but imagine if a teammate had corrected my first few steps after I rounded first base that day. Had that person offered me a course correction, I wouldn't have found myself in shallow centerfield.

This course correction is what God has called us to do as parents. He has given us the responsibility and privilege of starting our kids in the correct direction—one that seeks to know, love, and live for God. We are to point them toward the next "base," abundant living in Christ. We walk with them part of the way, showing them the beauty of God and the gospel and how our destination is better than anything the world has to offer. We also warn them of the danger and traps of the world: "There are thorns and snares on the way of the crooked; the one who guards himself stays far from them" (Proverbs 22:5).

The path toward godly living is beautiful and safe but not necessarily easy or pain free. It is a narrow path with fewer traveling on it than the broad path that leads to destruction (Matthew 7:13-14). Our kids need our help to know this path and travel it well.

The destination matters, but so does the journey.

As I played kickball, *why* I was running was just as important as *where* I was running. I wasn't running without reason; I was running as part of a larger, more meaningful story. I was playing a game and having fun with friends and my sons. The destination of reaching second base was important in the moment, but so was the purpose of my running.

As parents, we need to remember the bigger story of *why* we are pointing our kids in the right direction. It isn't merely to avoid problems and please God; it is so our kids can know God fully along the way—to find joy in the journey itself.

The best way to show our kids this correct path of life is by delighting in God in the normal, everyday rhythms of life. Yes, structured times of discipling our children are essential—this book helps with that. But it is just as important, perhaps even more, to show them how to weave God into our lives each day, or to put it more accurately, how to weave our daily lives around Him. We want to show how everything we do is designed to help us know and love God more than we did when we woke up that morning. Those organic conversations about God will carry over throughout the week and make it easier to recognize ideas and themes that spark more conversations about Him.

Your kids' journeys start with knowing God.

If we want our kids to walk along the correct path of living for Christ, it all begins with knowing who God is in the first place.

Cornerstones: 200 Questions and Answers to Learn Truth is designed to help kids learn the foundational doctrines of the Christian faith—not with the goal of knowing more about God, but instead to know God more. Each question and answer is designed to help explain who God is, how we can know Him better, and why He does what He does. *Cornerstones* teaches through questions and answers, a method that began in the early days of the church. The practice recognizes a child's natural inquisitive nature and offers doctrine in bite-size morsels. As kids understand each question and answer, they begin to develop a comprehensive understanding of God that deepens their love for Him. God moves from being a distant, unknown authority figure to a close, known, loving Father.

That is why this book is called *Cornerstones*. That title might seem odd at first because buildings have only one cornerstone—the stone that sets the horizontal and vertical directions for the rest of the structure. But whereas our faith has one ultimate Cornerstone in Jesus (Ephesians 2:20), having a proper understanding of God comes from rightly understanding many different truths about Him. Each of these truths are cornerstones in their own way, woven together in a beautiful tapestry to provide the right way for us to see God and learn to live for Him.

So how do I use this book?

You might consider picking up the companion book, *Cornerstones: 200 Questions and Answers to Teach Truth (Parent Guide)*. It provides helpful explanations and supporting Scriptures for the same questions and answers in this book for kids. Your goal is not merely to have your kids memorize the questions and answers but for them to understand the truths behind them as well. The Parent Guide equips you to have those meaningful conversations.

Think of two different "wins" for this book. The first is to have this book in your kids' hands as much as possible. It was designed to be engaging for them, so add it to their regular reading mix. Develop a rhythm where each child looks through part of the book—a few pages for younger kids and perhaps a chapter for older ones—and works to memorize the answer for each question they read. Two hundred questions may feel intimidating, but readers will get there over time.

The second win for this book is family discussions. A few times a week during dinner, my wife and I ask our kids these questions, see if they know the answers, and discuss them. We target the easier questions for our youngest son and the harder ones for our older two children. Sometimes one of the kids will ask the questions instead. Although learning about God is serious, we welcome humor and fun so that our kids equate learning about God with joyful, meaningful times.

Beyond dinnertime, try Saturday-morning breakfast, Thursday-night ice cream, or the ride to school each day—whatever fits your family's schedule. Look for opportunities to weave the questions and answers into daily life. If your child shows you an odd-looking bug in the yard, ask, "Who made everything—including that bug?" When you need to correct your child for doing wrong, ask, "Is there anyone who does not sin?" to remind her that she is not alone in her disobedience to God. You will be surprised to see how many opportunities you have to talk about God each day.

I am grateful for your ministry as a parent, and I am praying for you as we disciple our children. Remember, we aren't pointing our kids to something inconsequential such as second base, but to Jesus Christ! There is no greater ministry than showing them the way to know God, love God, and live for God found in Jesus each day.

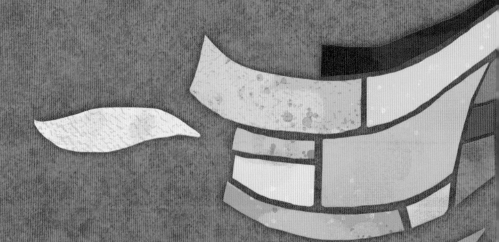

GOD

*May the Lord make
his face shine on you.*
—Numbers 6:25

*In the beginning God created
the heavens and the earth.*
—Genesis 1:1

1

Q. **What is God?**

A. God is creator and ruler
of everything.

2

Q. **Can we know that God exists?**

A. Yes, we can know that God exists from evidence in nature and in the Bible and from an inner sense that tells us He does.

3

Q. **How many gods are there?**

A. There is one true God, and only He deserves worship.

4

Q. **In how many Persons does God exist?**

A. God is one God in three Persons.

5

Q. **Who are the three Persons of God?**

A. The three Persons of God are
God the Father, God the Son,
and God the Holy Spirit.

6

Q. **Can we know the one true God?**

A. Yes, we can know the one true God
because He has revealed Himself to
us and He wants us to know Him.

7

Q. **How can we know God?**

A. God has revealed Himself to us through general revelation and special revelation.

8

Q. **What is general revelation?**

A. General revelation is God revealing Himself to everyone through His creation.

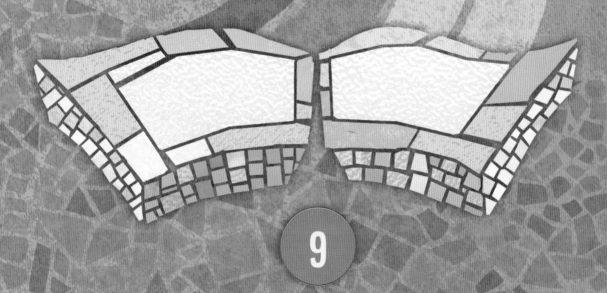

The instruction of the LORD is perfect, renewing one's life.
—Psalm 19:7

9

Q. **What is special revelation?**

A. Special revelation is God revealing Himself directly to people through the Bible.

10

Q. **What can we know about God?**

A. We can know what God is like, what He wants, and how we can have a relationship with Him.

11

Q. **Can we fully know God?**

A. No, we can know much about God, but we cannot fully know Him because of our limited minds.

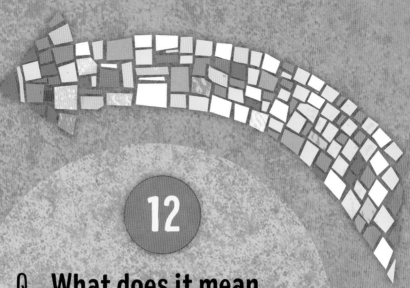

12

Q. **What does it mean that God is eternal?**

A. *God is eternal* means He has always existed and always will exist.

Before the mountains were born,
before you gave birth to the earth and the world,
from eternity to eternity, you are God.
—*Psalm 90:2*

13

Q. **What does it mean that God is a Person?**

A. *God is a Person* means He demonstrates intellect, emotion, and will.

"For my thoughts are not your thoughts, and your ways are not my ways."
—Isaiah 55:8

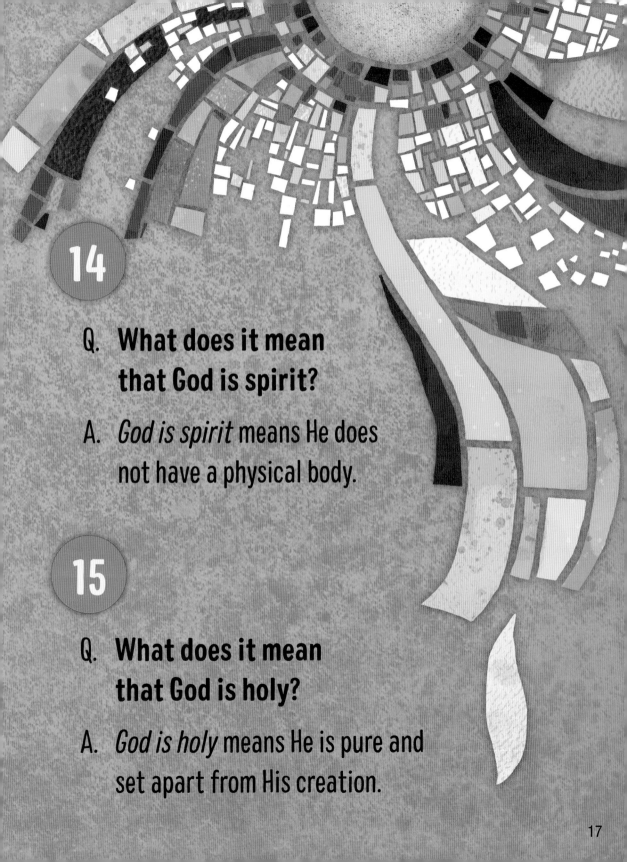

14

Q. **What does it mean that God is spirit?**

A. *God is spirit* means He does not have a physical body.

15

Q. **What does it mean that God is holy?**

A. *God is holy* means He is pure and set apart from His creation.

16

Q. **What does it mean that God is love?**

A. *God is love* means He expresses faithful love in all He does and He is the standard of love.

We love because he first loved us.
—1 John 4:19

17

Q. **What does it mean that God is just?**

A. *God is just* means He always acts in ways that are right and He is the standard of justice.

18

Q. **What does it mean that God is good?**

A. *God is good* means all He speaks and does is good and He is the standard of good.

19

Q. **What does it mean that God is true?**

A. *God is true* means all He speaks and does is true and He is the standard of truth.

20

Q. **What does it mean that God is wise?**

A. *God is wise* means He always wants and does what is best and He is the standard of wisdom.

*If we are faithless, he remains faithful,
for he cannot deny himself.
—2 Timothy 2:13*

21

Q. **What does it mean that God is faithful?**

A. *God is faithful* means He keeps His promises even when we are not faithful to Him.

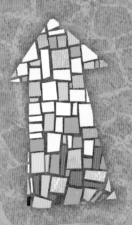

22

Q. **What does it mean that God is omnipresent?**

A. *God is omnipresent* means He is not confined to a body and is everywhere at once.

23

Q. **What does it mean
that God is omniscient?**

A. *God is omniscient* means
He knows all that is, was,
will be, and could be.

24

Q. **What does it mean
that God is omnipotent?**

A. *God is omnipotent* means
He can do anything that
is according to His
character.

Q. What does it mean that God is infinite?

A. *God is infinite* means He is limitless in all His attributes.

Our Lord is great, vast in power;
his understanding is infinite.
—Psalm 147:5

26

Q. **What does it mean that God is immutable?**

A. *God is immutable* means He does not change in who He is, His purposes, or His promises.

27

Q. **Is God perfect?**

A. Yes, God is perfect in all of His attributes, and He lacks nothing.

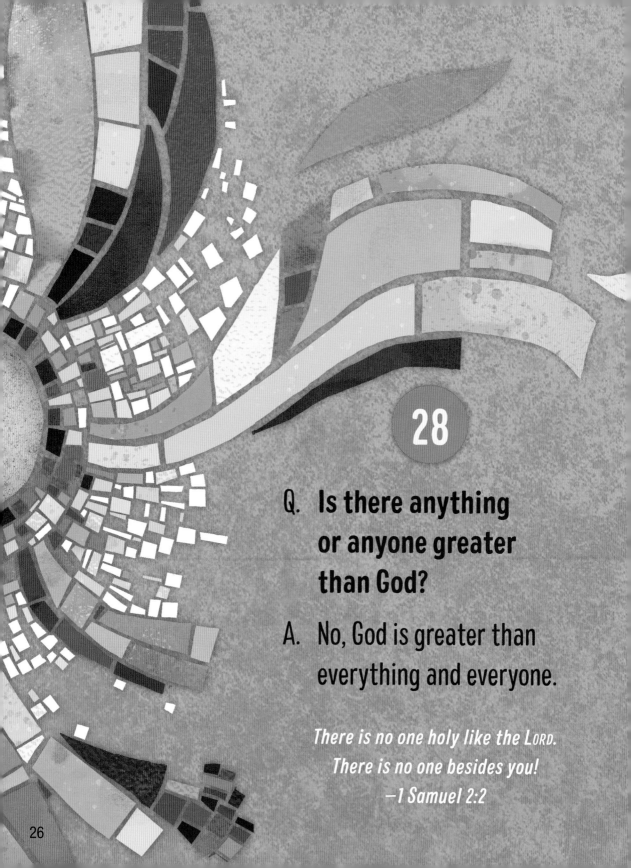

28

Q. **Is there anything or anyone greater than God?**

A. No, God is greater than everything and everyone.

There is no one holy like the Lord.
There is no one besides you!
—1 Samuel 2:2

29

Q. How much authority does God have?

A. God is a sovereign ruler and has total authority over everything.

30

Q. What is God's providence?

A. God's providence is how He works with people and His creation to bring about what He wants.

CREATION

By faith we understand that
the universe was created by the word
of God, so that what is seen was made
from things that are not visible.
—Hebrews 11:3

Now the earth was formless and empty, darkness covered the surface of the watery depths, and the Spirit of God was hovering over the surface of the waters.
—Genesis 1:2

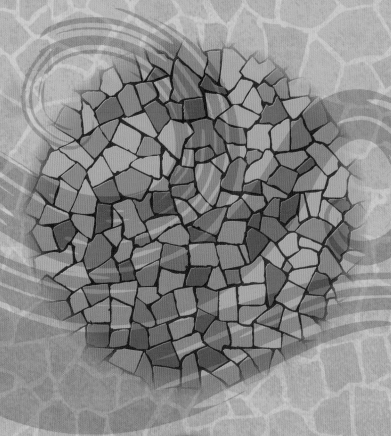

1

Q. Who created everything?

A. God created the world and everything else in the universe.

2

Q. **Why did God create everything?**

A. God created everything for His glory.

3

Q. **How did God create everything?**

A. God created everything by His spoken word.

In the beginning was the Word, and the Word was with God, and the Word was God.
—John 1:1

4

Q. **In what condition was everything God created?**

A. God created everything perfectly good.

5

Q. **How does God rule over His creation?**

A. God rules over His creation perfectly and with loving care according to His purposes.

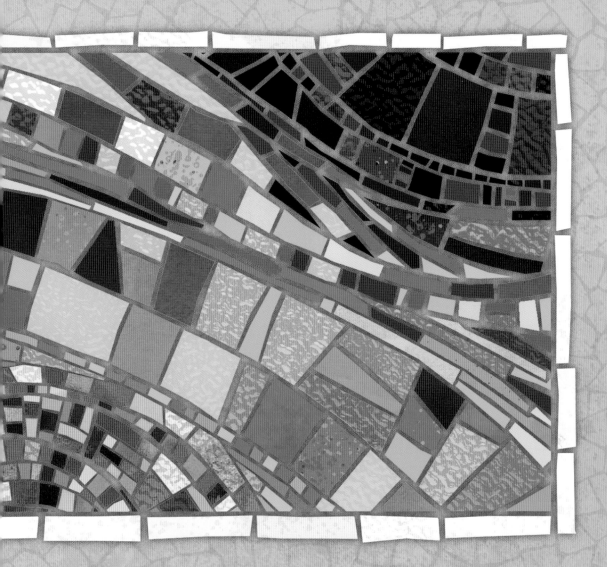

6

Q. What did God create on the first day?

A. On the first day, God created light and formed day and night.

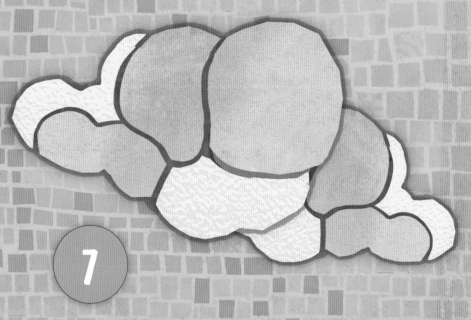

7

Q. What did God create on the second day?

A. On the second day,
God created the sky.

Then God said, "Let there be an expanse between the waters, separating water from water."
—Genesis 1:6

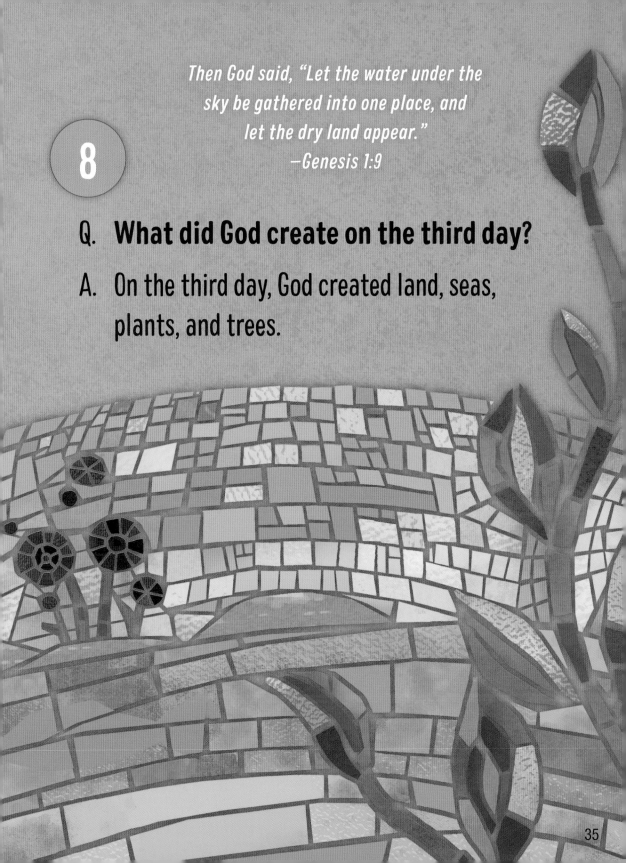

8

Then God said, "Let the water under the sky be gathered into one place, and let the dry land appear."
—Genesis 1:9

Q. **What did God create on the third day?**

A. On the third day, God created land, seas, plants, and trees.

9

Q. **What did God create on the fourth day?**

A. On the fourth day, God created the sun, moon, and stars.

Then God said, "Let there be lights in the expanse of the sky to separate the day from the night."
—Genesis 1:14

Then God said, "Let the water swarm with living creatures, and let birds fly above the earth across the expanse of the sky."
—Genesis 1:20

10

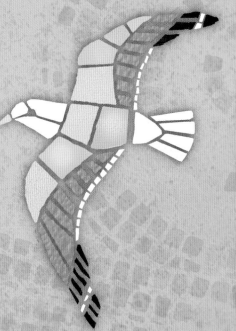

Q. **What did God create on the fifth day?**

A. On the fifth day, God created birds and sea creatures.

Then God said, "Let us make man in our image, according to our likeness. They will rule the fish of the sea, the birds of the sky, the livestock, the whole earth, and the creatures that crawl on the earth."
—Genesis 1:26

11

Q. **What did God create on the sixth day?**

A. On the sixth day, God created animals and people.

12

Q. What did God create on the seventh day?

A. On the seventh day, God rested.

God blessed the seventh day and
declared it holy, for on it he rested from
all his work of creation.
—Genesis 2:3

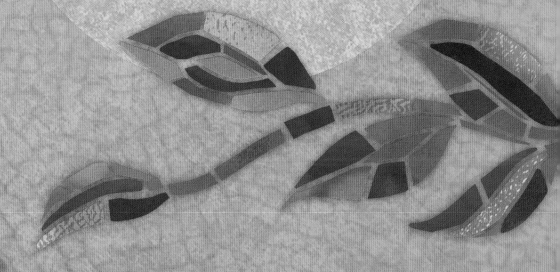

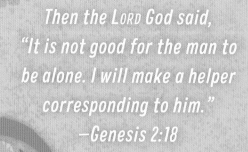

Then the Lord God said,
"It is not good for the man to
be alone. I will make a helper
corresponding to him."
—Genesis 2:18

13

Q. Who were the first people God created?

A. God created Adam and Eve as the first man and woman.

14

Q. **How did God create Adam and Eve?**

A. God formed Adam from the dust of the ground and breathed life into him, and God created Eve from Adam's rib.

41

Q. **In what way did God create Adam and Eve?**

A. God created Adam and Eve as male and female, each in His own image.

So God created man in his own image;
he created him in the image of God;
he created them male and female.
—Genesis 1:27

16

Q. **What did God give Adam and Eve besides a body?**

A. God gave Adam and Eve a spirit so they could know Him.

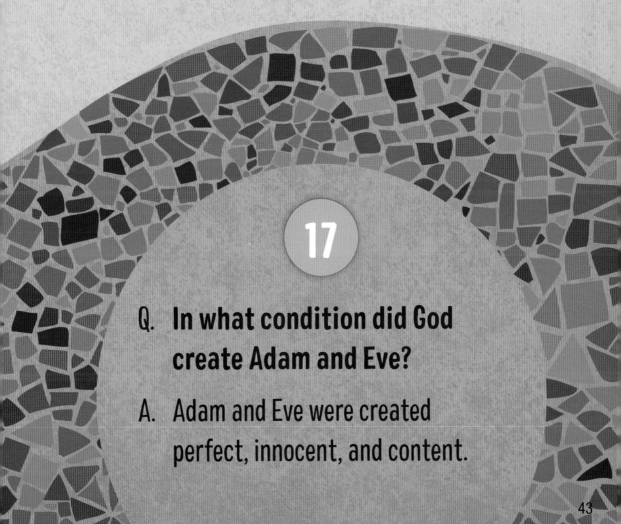

17

Q. **In what condition did God create Adam and Eve?**

A. Adam and Eve were created perfect, innocent, and content.

18

Q. **Why did God create Adam and Eve?**

A. God created Adam and Eve and all people to love Him, worship Him, and give Him glory.

19

Q. **What were Adam and Eve to do?**

A. Adam and Eve were to rule over creation and start a family.

We love because he first loved us.
—1 John 4:19

20

Q. **What command did God give Adam and Eve?**

A. God commanded Adam and Eve not to eat from the tree of the knowledge of good and evil.

SIN

And the LORD God commanded the man, "You are free to eat from any tree of the garden, but you must not eat from the tree of the knowledge of good and evil, for on the day you eat from it, you will certainly die."
—Genesis 2:16-17

Q. Did Adam and Eve remain perfect, innocent, and content?

A. No, Adam and Eve disobeyed God's command not to eat from the tree of the knowledge of good and evil. This was the first sin.

2

Q. Why did Adam and Eve eat the fruit from the tree of the knowledge of good and evil?

A. The devil tricked Eve. She wanted to be like God, so she ate the fruit, and so did Adam.

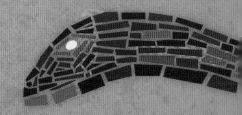

"Did God really say, 'You can't eat from any tree in the garden'?"
—Genesis 3:1

3

Q. Who is the devil?

A. The devil, also called Satan, is a fallen angel who wants to take glory from God.

4

Q. How does the devil try to take glory from God?

A. The devil tries to take glory from God by lying, stealing, killing, and destroying.

Be sober-minded, be alert. Your adversary the devil is prowling around like a roaring lion, looking for anyone he can devour.
—1 Peter 5:8

5

Q. Will the devil win against God?

A. No, the devil has already lost and will be judged by God one day.

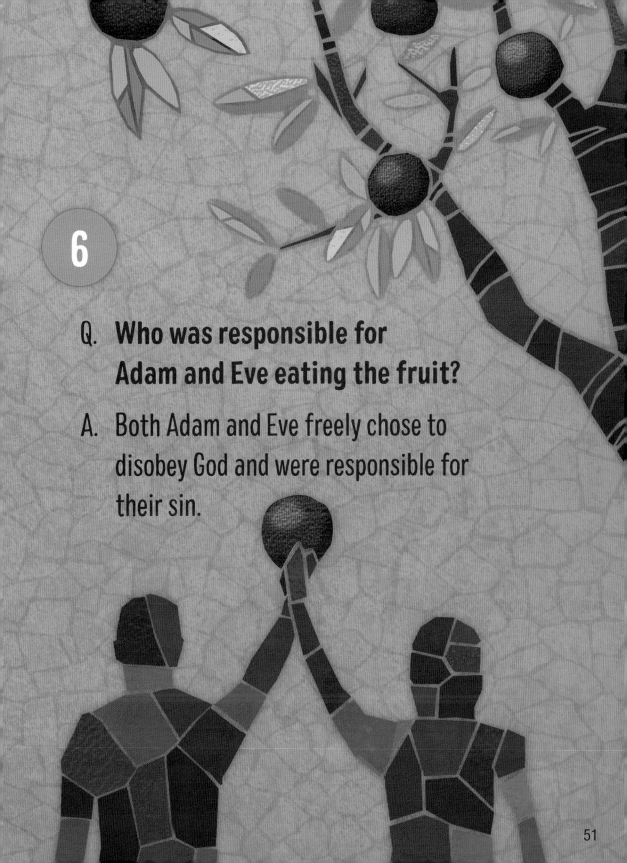

6

Q. **Who was responsible for Adam and Eve eating the fruit?**

A. Both Adam and Eve freely chose to disobey God and were responsible for their sin.

7

Q. **What happened to Adam and Eve when they disobeyed God?**

A. Adam and Eve became sinful and separated from God when they disobeyed Him.

8

Q. What did God say would happen to the serpent for its part in the first sin?

A. God said the serpent would be cursed more than any other animal.

So the Lord God said to the serpent:
Because you have done this,
you are cursed more than any livestock
and more than any wild animal.
You will move on your belly
and eat dust all the days of your life.
—Genesis 3:14

9

Q. **What did God say would happen to Eve for her part in the first sin?**

A. God said Eve would have increased pain giving birth and her relationship with Adam would become difficult.

10

Q. **What did God say would happen to Adam for his part in the first sin?**

A. God said Adam would have to work hard to produce food to eat.

11

Q. **What did God promise Adam and Eve would happen one day?**

A. God promised Adam and Eve that one of their offspring would strike the head of the serpent one day.

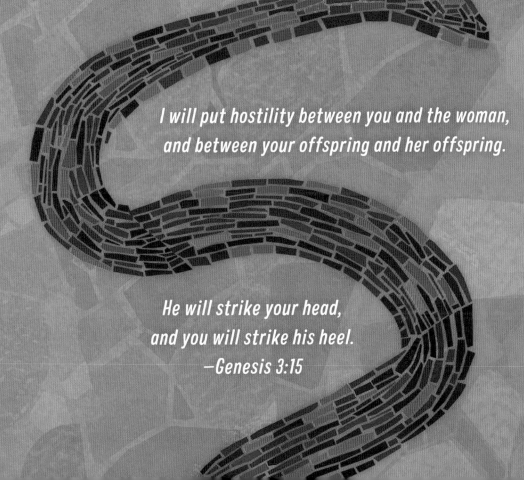

I will put hostility between you and the woman, and between your offspring and her offspring.

He will strike your head, and you will strike his heel.
—Genesis 3:15

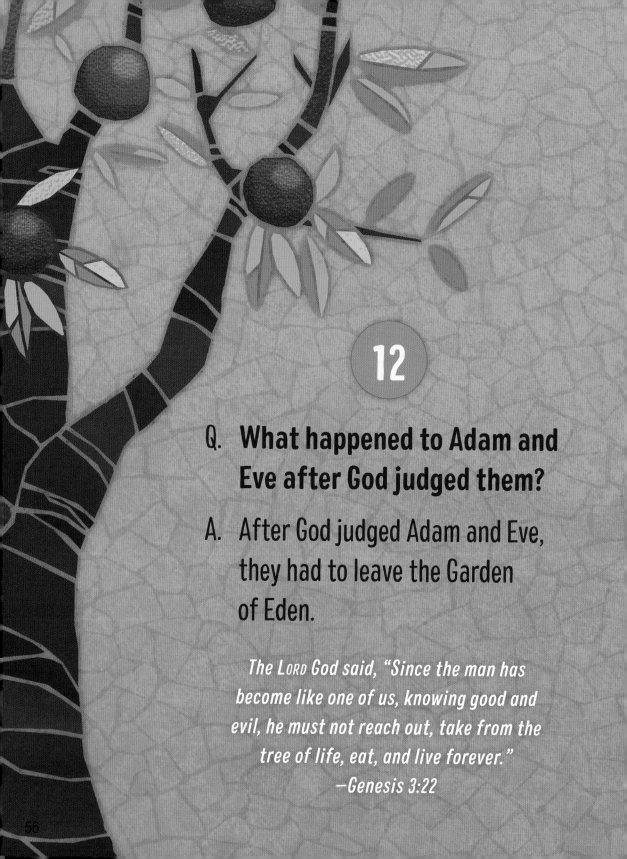

12

Q. **What happened to Adam and Eve after God judged them?**

A. After God judged Adam and Eve, they had to leave the Garden of Eden.

The Lᴏʀᴅ God said, "Since the man has become like one of us, knowing good and evil, he must not reach out, take from the tree of life, eat, and live forever."
—Genesis 3:22

13

Q. What effect did Adam's and Eve's sin have on all people?

A. Because of Adam's and Eve's sin, all people since have been born with a sin nature.

14

Q. What effect did Adam's and Eve's sin have on all of creation?

A. Because of Adam's and Eve's sin, all of creation has been cursed and is no longer as it should be.

15

Q. What is sin?

A. Sin is disobeying God by doing what He forbids, not doing what He commands, or not having the right attitude toward Him or others.

16

Q. **Where does sin begin?**

A. Sin begins in the heart, where we choose not to fulfill our created purpose to love, worship, and glorify God as He deserves.

17

Q. **Is there anyone who does not sin?**

A. No, everyone sins.

So it is sin to know the good and yet not do it.
—James 4:17

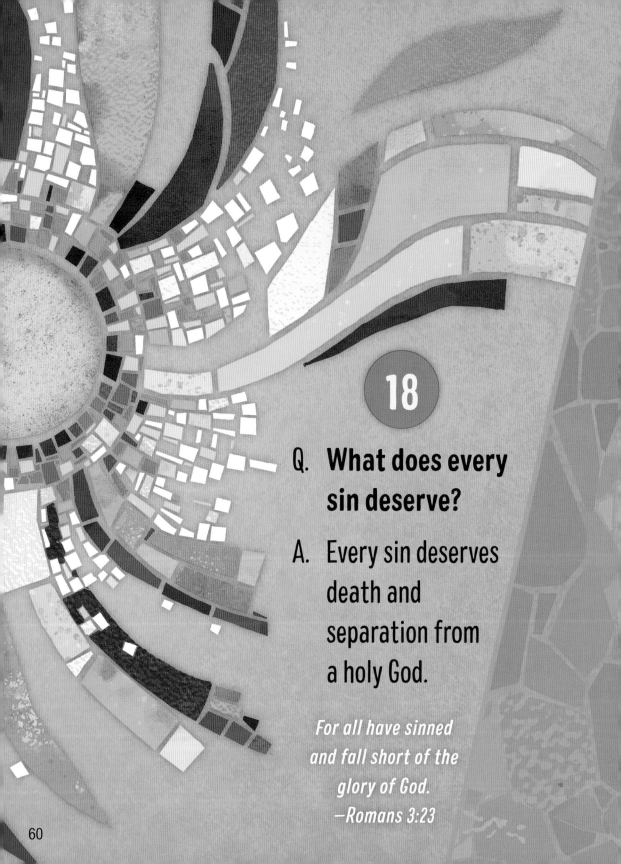

18

Q. **What does every sin deserve?**

A. Every sin deserves death and separation from a holy God.

For all have sinned and fall short of the glory of God.
—Romans 3:23

19

Q. How does sin impact a person's relationship with God?

A. Because God is perfect, no one can be sinful and have a relationship with God.

20

Q. Do people have to die and stay separated from God because of sin?

A. No, God has provided a way to be forgiven of sin, to be saved from death, and to enjoy a relationship with Him.

JESUS

*"For God loved the world in this way:
He gave his one and only Son, so that
everyone who believes in him will not
perish but have eternal life."*
—John 3:16

1

Q. How can a person be saved from sin and have eternal life with God?

A. Only through faith in God the Son can a person be saved from sin and receive eternal life with God.

If you confess with your mouth, "Jesus is Lord," and believe in your heart that God raised him from the dead, you will be saved.
—Romans 10:9

2

Q. Has God the Son always existed?

A. Yes, God the Son has always existed, just as the Father and the Holy Spirit have.

3

Q. **By what other name
do we know God the Son?**

A. We also know God the Son
as Jesus.

Q. **Is Jesus God or man?**

A. Jesus is both fully God and fully man.

5

Q. **Why did God the Son become human?**

A. God the Son became human to please the Father and provide forgiveness of sin.

"I have glorified you on the earth by completing the work you gave me to do."
—John 17:4

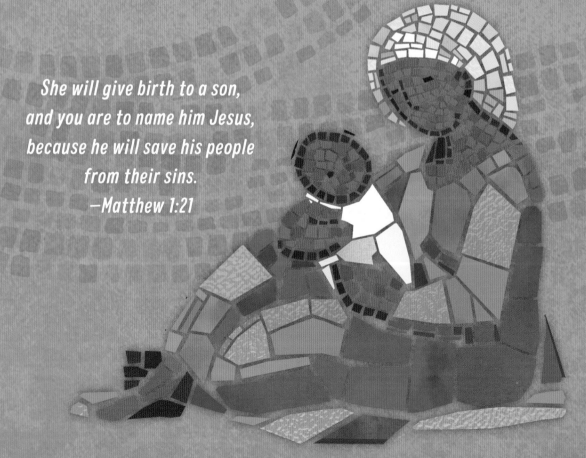

6

Q. **How was Jesus born?**

A. Jesus was born of the virgin Mary.

*She will give birth to a son,
and you are to name him Jesus,
because he will save his people
from their sins.
—Matthew 1:21*

7

Q. **Why was Jesus born of a virgin?**

A. Jesus was born of a virgin to reveal He is the Son of God and to protect Him from inheriting a sinful nature.

> *You know that he was revealed so that he might take away sins, and there is no sin in him.*
> —1 John 3:5

8

Q. **What title is given to Jesus?**

A. Jesus is given the title of Christ, or the Messiah.

9

Q. **What did Jesus do while He was on earth?**

A. While Jesus was on earth, He traveled through Galilee, Samaria, and Judea teaching and performing miracles.

And there are also many other things that Jesus did, which, if every one of them were written down, I suppose not even the world itself could contain the books that would be written.
—John 21:25

10

Q. **What did Jesus teach when He was on earth?**

A. Jesus taught about who God is, God's kingdom, and how to live in a way that brings God glory.

11

Q. Why did Jesus perform miracles?

A. Jesus performed miracles to glorify God, to prove He is the Son of God, and because He loves people.

12

Q. **What three offices does Jesus fulfill?**

A. Jesus is the perfect fulfillment of the offices of Prophet, Priest, and King.

13

Q. How does Jesus perfectly fulfill the office of Prophet?

A. Jesus perfectly revealed the Father to us and was the fulfillment of what all the other prophets spoke.

> *The LORD your God will raise up for you a prophet like me from among your own brothers.*
> *—Deuteronomy 18:15*

14

Q. How does Jesus perfectly fulfill the office of Priest?

A. Jesus was the perfect sacrifice made for us and continues to intercede to the Father on our behalf as our great High Priest.

15

Q. How does Jesus perfectly fulfill the office of King?

A. Jesus perfectly reigns over His people as King of kings.

16

Q. What did Jesus do to provide forgiveness of sin?

A. Jesus provided forgiveness of sin by living a perfect life and dying on the cross to pay the punishment for sin.

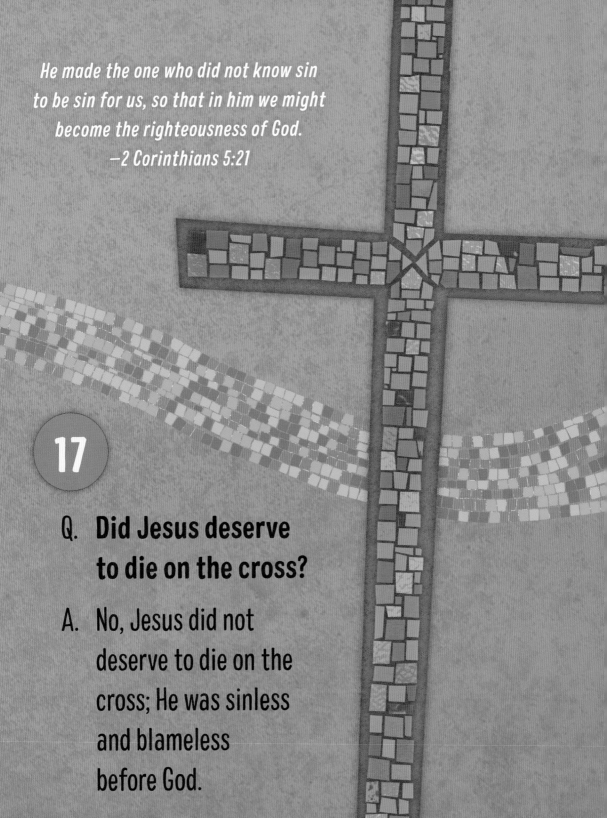

He made the one who did not know sin to be sin for us, so that in him we might become the righteousness of God.
—2 Corinthians 5:21

17

Q. **Did Jesus deserve to die on the cross?**

A. No, Jesus did not deserve to die on the cross; He was sinless and blameless before God.

18

Q. **What happened on the third day after Jesus was crucified?**

A. On the third day, Jesus rose from the dead and left the grave.

19

Q. **Is there any evidence that Jesus rose from the dead?**

A. Yes, many witnesses saw Jesus after He rose from the dead.

After he had said this, he was taken up as they were watching, and a cloud took him out of their sight.
—Acts 1:9

20

Q. **Where is Jesus now?**

A. Forty days after Jesus rose, He ascended into heaven to return to His place of glory with the Father where He will remain until His return.

SALVATION

"If I go away and prepare a place for you, I will come again and take you to myself, so that where I am you may be also."
—John 14:3

1

Q. **What does it mean to be righteous?**

A. *To be righteous* is to obey God fully and live in a way that pleases Him.

> All a person's ways seem right to him,
> but the LORD weighs hearts.
> —Proverbs 21:2

2

Q. **Can anyone be saved by his or her own righteousness?**

A. No, no one is righteous enough to be saved.

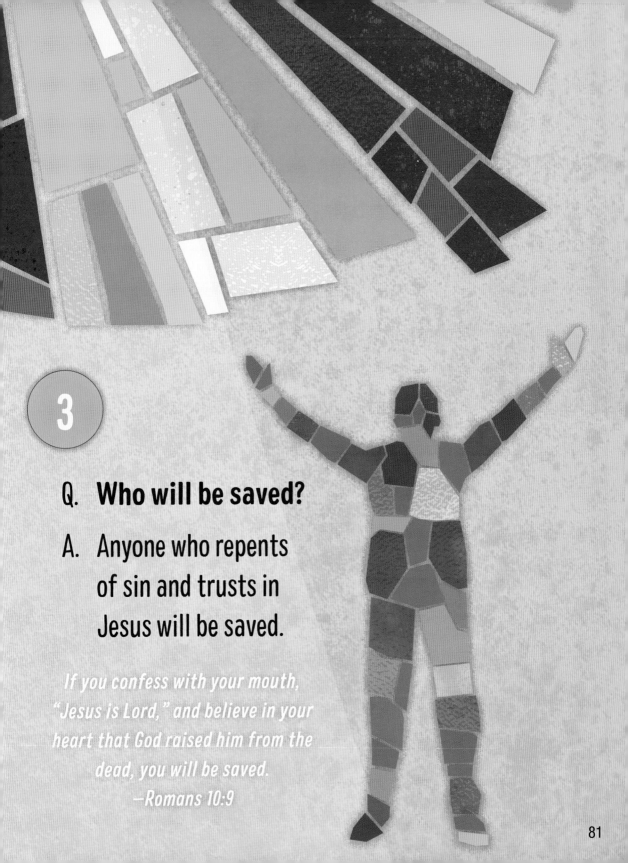

3

Q. **Who will be saved?**

A. Anyone who repents of sin and trusts in Jesus will be saved.

If you confess with your mouth, "Jesus is Lord," and believe in your heart that God raised him from the dead, you will be saved.
—Romans 10:9

4

Q. How were people saved before Jesus came to earth?

A. People were saved by faith that God would provide Jesus one day.

Abram believed the LORD, and he credited it to him as righteousness.
—Genesis 15:6

5

Q. How did people in the Old Testament show their faith that God would forgive their sin?

A. People in the Old Testament showed their faith in God by offering animal sacrifices to Him.

6

Q. **What did the animal sacrifices represent?**

A. The animal sacrifices represented Jesus, the perfect sacrifice who was to come.

According to the law almost everything is purified with blood, and without the shedding of blood there is no forgiveness.
—Hebrews 9:22

7

Q. How did Jesus being fully human make it possible for people to be saved?

A. Because Jesus is fully human, He was able to die the death sin deserves.

8

Q. How did Jesus being fully God make it possible for people to be saved?

A. Because Jesus is fully God, He was able to be the perfect sacrifice for the sins of the world.

"Just as the Son of Man did not come to be served, but to serve, and to give his life as a ransom for many."
—Matthew 20:28

9

Q. **What does it mean to repent?**

A. *To repent* is to be grieved by sin and turn from it.

What should we say then? Should we continue in sin so that grace may multiply? Absolutely not! How can we who died to sin still live in it?
—Romans 6:1-2

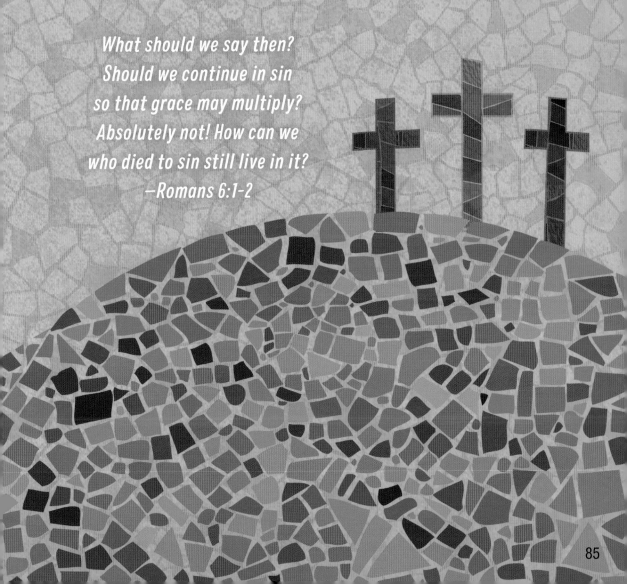

10

Q. What does it mean to trust in Jesus?

A. *To trust in Jesus* is to believe that Jesus is the Son of God, to have faith that He paid for your sin, and to love and follow Him.

If you confess with your mouth, "Jesus is Lord," and believe in your heart that God raised him from the dead, you will be saved.
—Romans 10:9

11

Q. **What is grace?**

A. *Grace* is God giving us good things that we do not deserve.

For you are saved by grace through faith, and this is not from yourselves; it is God's gift.
—Ephesians 2:8-9

12

Q. **What is mercy?**

A. *Mercy* is God not giving us punishment that we deserve.

13

Q. What is atonement?

A. *Atonement* is Jesus living a perfect life and paying our sin penalty to make us right with God.

14

Q. **What is regeneration?**

A. *Regeneration* is the Holy Spirit causing us to be born again, giving us new hearts that love God.

15

Q. **What is justification?**

A. *Justification* is God declaring that we are forgiven of our sins and that we are righteous.

They are justified freely by his grace through the redemption that is in Christ Jesus.
—Romans 3:24

16

Q. **What is adoption?**

A. *Adoption* is God bringing us into His family as His children.

17

Q. **What is sanctification?**

A. *Sanctification* is where we gradually grow to live more like Jesus.

18

Q. What is glorification?

A. *Glorification* is when believers will be made completely right and perfect again in the restored creation.

You did not receive a spirit of slavery to fall back into fear. Instead, you received the Spirit of adoption, by whom we cry out, "Abba, Father!"
—Romans 8:15

19

Q. What does Jesus take from us and give us when we are saved?

A. When we are saved, Jesus takes our sin and gives us His righteousness.

He made the one who did not know sin to be sin for us, so that in him we might become the righteousness of God.
—2 Corinthians 5:21

20

Q. **Can someone who has truly trusted in Christ fall away from God?**

A. No, all true Christians persevere to the end.

"I give them eternal life, and they will never perish. No one will snatch them out of my hand."
—John 10:28

The BIBLE

The revelation of your words brings light and gives understanding to the inexperienced.
—Psalm 119:130

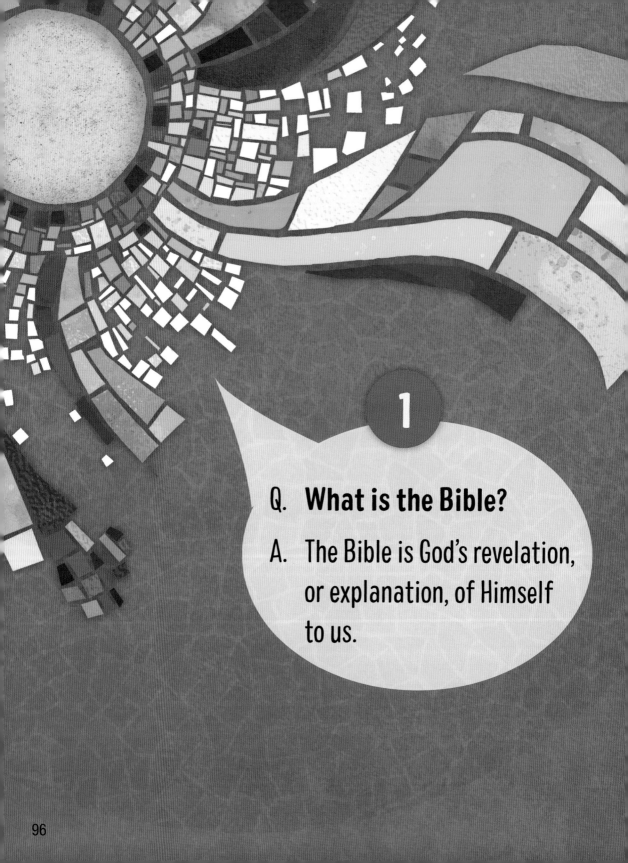

1

Q. **What is the Bible?**

A. The Bible is God's revelation, or explanation, of Himself to us.

2

Q. **Who wrote the Bible?**

A. Men who were inspired by the Holy Spirit wrote the Bible.

All Scripture is inspired by God and is profitable for teaching, for rebuking, for correcting, for training in righteousness.
—2 Timothy 3:16

3

Q. **What does inspiration mean?**

A. *Inspiration* is God moving the writers of Scripture to write what He wanted them to write.

4

Q. **Is the Bible true?**

A. Yes, the Bible is true and has no error.

"Sanctify them by the truth; your word is truth."
—John 17:17

5

Q. **How is the Bible true if it was written by men?**

A. The Holy Spirit guided the process of men writing the Bible to protect it from error.

6

Q. How is the Bible organized?

A. The Bible contains 66 books—39 in the Old Testament and 27 in the New Testament.

7

Q. **What are the five divisions of the Old Testament?**

A. The Old Testament is made up of the law, history, writings, major prophets, and minor prophets.

8

Q. What is the difference between the major and minor prophets?

A. The difference between the major and minor prophets is the length of the books, not their importance.

9

Q. What are the five divisions of the New Testament?

A. The New Testament is made up of the Gospels, history, Pauline epistles, general epistles, and prophecy.

10

Q. **What is an epistle?**

A. *An epistle* is a letter, usually written to local churches in different cities.

11

Q. **What is the Bible about?**

A. The Bible is the story of God providing Jesus to save us from our sin.

12

Q. **What else does the Bible teach us?**

A. The Bible teaches us how we can live to please God.

All Scripture is inspired by God and is profitable for teaching, for rebuking, for correcting, for training in righteousness, so that the man of God may be complete, equipped for every good work.
—2 Timothy 3:16-17

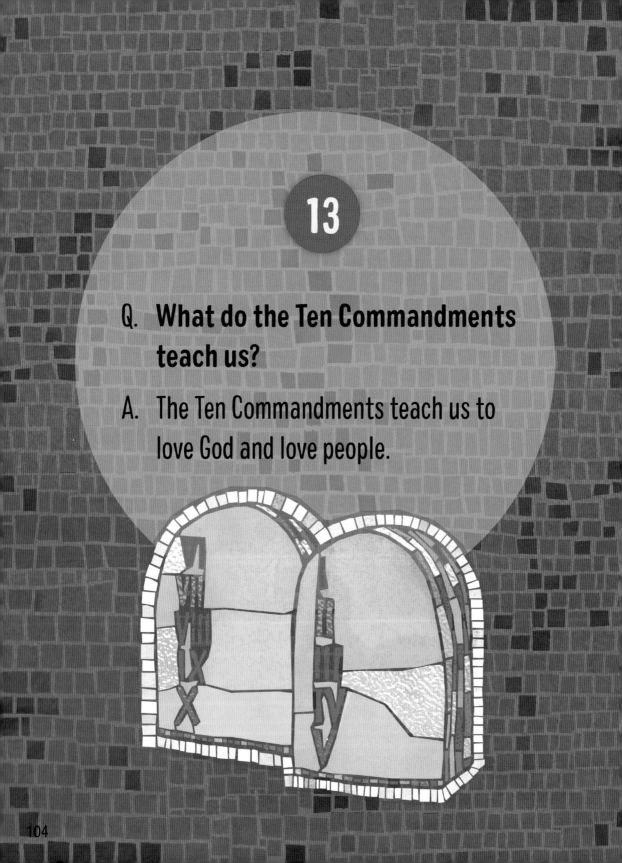

13

Q. **What do the Ten Commandments teach us?**

A. The Ten Commandments teach us to love God and love people.

14

Q. **What are the first four commandments about?**

A. The first four commandments are about our relationship with God.

Love the Lᴏʀᴅ your God with all your heart, with all your soul, and with all your strength.
—Deuteronomy 6:5

15

Q. **What are the last six commandments about?**

A. The last six commandments are about our relationships with others.

16

Q. What is the first commandment?

A. The first commandment is to have no gods other than God.

17

Q. What is the second commandment?

A. The second commandment is not to make or worship idols.

18

Q. **What is the third commandment?**

A. The third commandment is not to misuse the Lord's name.

19

Q. **What is the fourth commandment?**

A. The fourth commandment is to remember the Sabbath to keep it holy.

20

Q. **What is the fifth commandment?**

A. The fifth commandment is to honor your father and mother.

21

Q. **What is the sixth commandment?**

A. The sixth commandment is not to murder.

22

Q. **What is the seventh commandment?**

A. The seventh commandment is not to commit adultery.

23

Q. **What is the eighth commandment?**

A. The eighth commandment is not to steal.

24

Q. **What is the ninth commandment?**

A. The ninth commandment is not to give false testimony.

25

Q. **What is the tenth commandment?**

A. The tenth commandment is not to covet things that don't belong to us.

26

Q. **Can anyone obey the Ten Commandments and the Law?**

A. No, no one can obey the Ten Commandments and the Law because of our sin.

For whoever keeps the entire law, and yet stumbles at one point, is guilty of breaking it all.
—James 2:10

27

Q. **What is the main purpose of the Ten Commandments and the Old Testament Law?**

A. The Ten Commandments and the Law show us God's standard of obedience and reveal our sin and need of grace.

28

Q. **What did Jesus say is the greatest commandment?**

A. Jesus said the greatest commandment is to love God.

He said to him, "Love the Lord your God with all your heart, with all your soul, and with all your mind. This is the greatest and most important command."
—Matthew 22:37-38

29

Q. **What did Jesus say is the second greatest commandment?**

A. Jesus said the second greatest commandment is to love others.

> *"The second is like it: Love your neighbor as yourself. All the Law and the Prophets depend on these two commands."*
> *—Matthew 22:39-40*

30

Q. **How do the first and second greatest commandments help us live for God?**

A. The first and second greatest commandments provide the purpose for all we do.

DISCIPLESHIP

"Follow me," he told them,
"and I will make you fish for people."
—Matthew 4:19

1

Q. **What is the purpose of our lives?**

A. The purpose of our lives is to glorify God in all we do.

2

Q. **Why should we glorify God?**

A. We should glorify God because He made us, loves us, takes care of us, and is perfect in all His attributes.

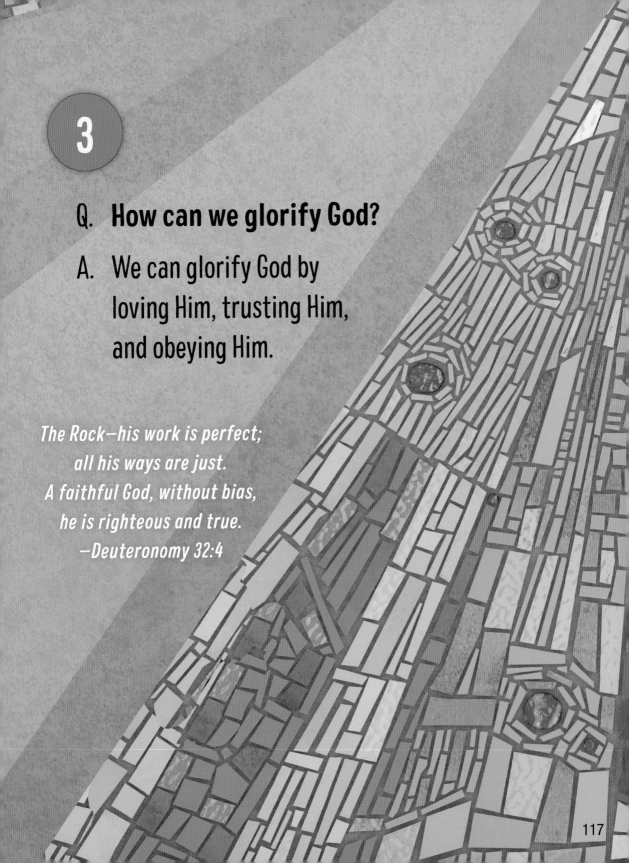

3

Q. **How can we glorify God?**

A. We can glorify God by loving Him, trusting Him, and obeying Him.

The Rock—his work is perfect;
all his ways are just.
A faithful God, without bias,
he is righteous and true.
—Deuteronomy 32:4

"If you love me, you will keep my commands."
—John 14:15

4

Q. **Why should we love God?**

A. We should love God because He first loved us.

5

Q. Why should we trust God?

A. We should trust God because He is faithful and everything He does is for His glory and our good.

We know that all things work together for the good of those who love God, who are called according to his purpose.
—Romans 8:28

6

Q. Why should we obey God?

A. We should obey God because we love Him and are thankful for who He is and what He has done.

7

Q. **Will we fully obey God during our lifetime?**

A. No, we will not fully obey God during our lifetime, but we should want to obey Him more each day.

8

Q. **What helps us obey God more?**

A. God helps us obey Him more by giving us wisdom, the ability to make choices that glorify Him.

Q. **Where does God's wisdom come from?**

A. God's wisdom comes from Him through His Word.

Now if any of you lacks wisdom, he should ask God—
who gives to all generously and ungrudgingly—
and it will be given to him.
—James 1:5

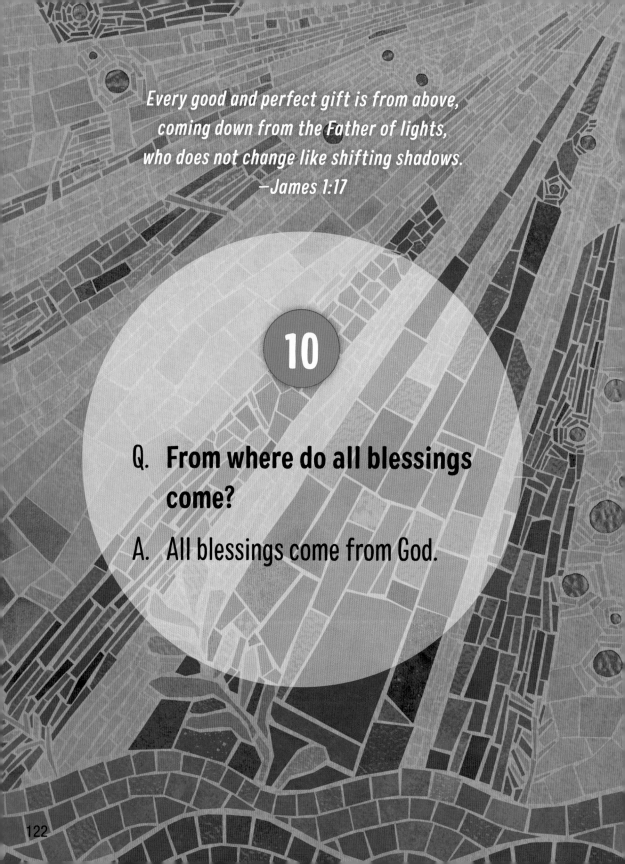

Every good and perfect gift is from above,
coming down from the Father of lights,
who does not change like shifting shadows.
—James 1:17

10

Q. **From where do all blessings come?**

A. All blessings come from God.

11

Q. **How has God blessed us?**

A. God has blessed us with life, talents, possessions, and salvation through Jesus.

12

Q. **Who owns all that we have?**

A. God owns all that we have, and we are His stewards.

"For God loved the world in this way: He gave his one and only Son, so that everyone who believes in him will not perish but have eternal life."
—John 3:16

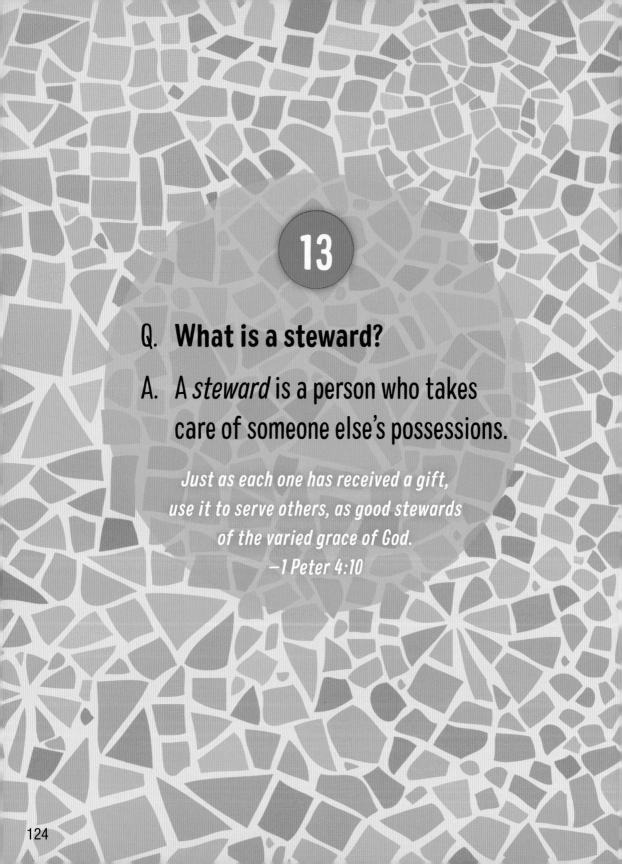

13

Q. **What is a steward?**

A. A *steward* is a person who takes care of someone else's possessions.

*Just as each one has received a gift,
use it to serve others, as good stewards
of the varied grace of God.*
—1 Peter 4:10

14

Q. **Why should we serve God as stewards?**

A. We should serve God as stewards to glorify Him and help others.

15

Q. **How should we give of our time, talents, and possessions as stewards?**

A. We should give of our time, talents, and possessions regularly, generously, and cheerfully.

16

Q. **What is our mission as Christians?**

A. Our mission as Christians is to make disciples of all nations by the power of the Holy Spirit.

"Go, therefore, and make disciples of all nations, baptizing them in the name of the Father and of the Son and of the Holy Spirit, teaching them to observe everything I have commanded you. And remember, I am with you always, to the end of the age."
—Matthew 28:19-20

17

Q. **Why should we seek to make disciples of Jesus?**

A. We should seek to make disciples of Jesus because it is our duty and privilege, and so that others may come to experience the joy of salvation.

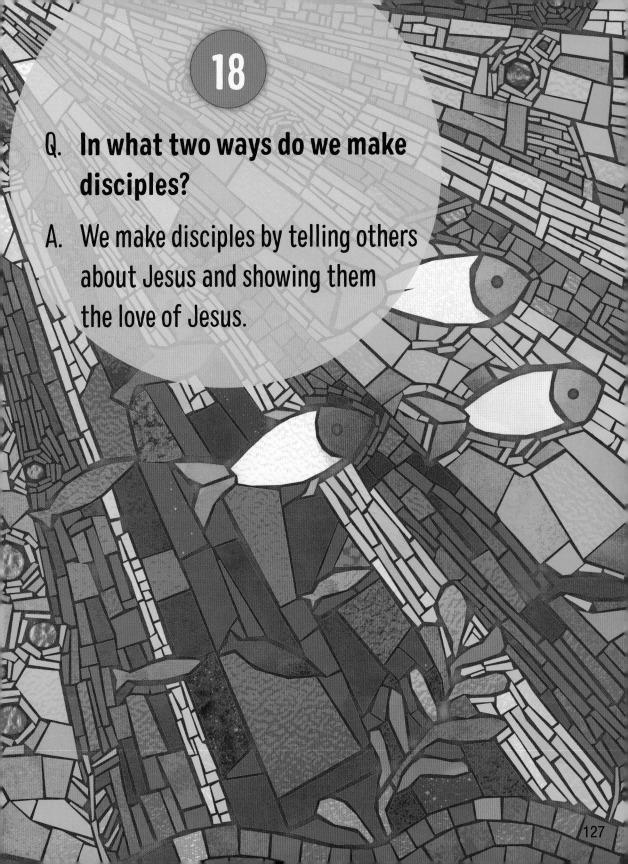

18

Q. **In what two ways do we make disciples?**

A. We make disciples by telling others about Jesus and showing them the love of Jesus.

19

Q. How should we feel about people who have not trusted in Jesus?

A. We should love and have compassion for those who have not trusted in Jesus.

20

Q. How much of the world should we want to see reached for Jesus?

A. We should want all the world—people from every nation, language, and ethnic group—to trust in Christ.

21

Q. What is the kingdom of God?

A. The *kingdom of God* is God's general rule over all of creation and His direct rule over those who have trusted in Jesus.

Your kingdom is an everlasting kingdom;
your rule is for all generations.
The Lord is faithful in all his words
and gracious in all his actions.
—Psalm 145:13

22

Q. **What should we pray for the kingdom?**

A. We should pray for God's kingdom to come and God's will to be done.

"Our Father in heaven,
your name be honored as holy.
Your kingdom come.
Your will be done
on earth as it is in heaven."
—Matthew 6:9-11

23

Q. **How should we live in an unjust world?**

A. We should live seeking to promote justice, defend the helpless, and oppose sin.

Mankind, he has told each of you what is good
and what it is the Lord requires of you:
to act justly, to love faithfulness,
and to walk humbly with your God.
—Micah 6:8

24

Q. **Do Christians continue to sin?**

A. Yes, Christians continue to sin, although all our sin is forgiven.

25

Q. **Do Christians have to sin?**

A. No, Christians can resist sin.

*Therefore, there is now no condemnation
for those in Christ Jesus.
—Romans 8:1*

26

Q. **How can Christians resist sin?**

A. Christians can resist sin through the power of the Holy Spirit, reading the Bible, and the encouragement of other Christians.

27

Q. **How does the Holy Spirit help us when we are worried, afraid, or sad?**

A. The Holy Spirit comforts us and gives us peace when we are worried, afraid, or sad.

*I have treasured your word in my heart
so that I may not sin against you.
—Psalm 119:11*

28

Q. **How does the Holy Spirit help us when we sin?**

A. The Holy Spirit helps us when we sin by convicting our hearts and helping us repent and turn back to God.

29

Q. **How does the Holy Spirit change us?**

A. The Holy Spirit changes us by reminding us of the truth of the gospel and making us more like Christ.

30

Q. **How does the Holy Spirit help us live for God?**

A. The Holy Spirit helps us to pray, read, and understand the Bible, and to obey God.

Now God has revealed these things to us by the Spirit, since the Spirit searches everything, even the depths of God.
—1 Corinthians 2:10

31

Q. **Is the Holy Spirit a Person?**

A. Yes, the Holy Spirit is a Person just like God the Father and God the Son.

32

Q. **Where is the Holy Spirit?**

A. The Holy Spirit lives in all Christians.

This hope will not disappoint us, because God's love has been poured out in our hearts through the Holy Spirit who was given to us.
—Romans 5:5

33

Q. **What is prayer?**

A. *Prayer* is talking with God.

34

Q.   **When do we pray?**

A.   We are to pray always.

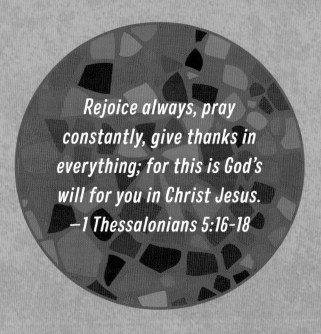

Rejoice always, pray constantly, give thanks in everything; for this is God's will for you in Christ Jesus.
—1 Thessalonians 5:16-18

35

Q.   **What are some of the things we share with God as we pray?**

A.   As we pray, we praise God, share our desires with Him, and confess our sins to Him.

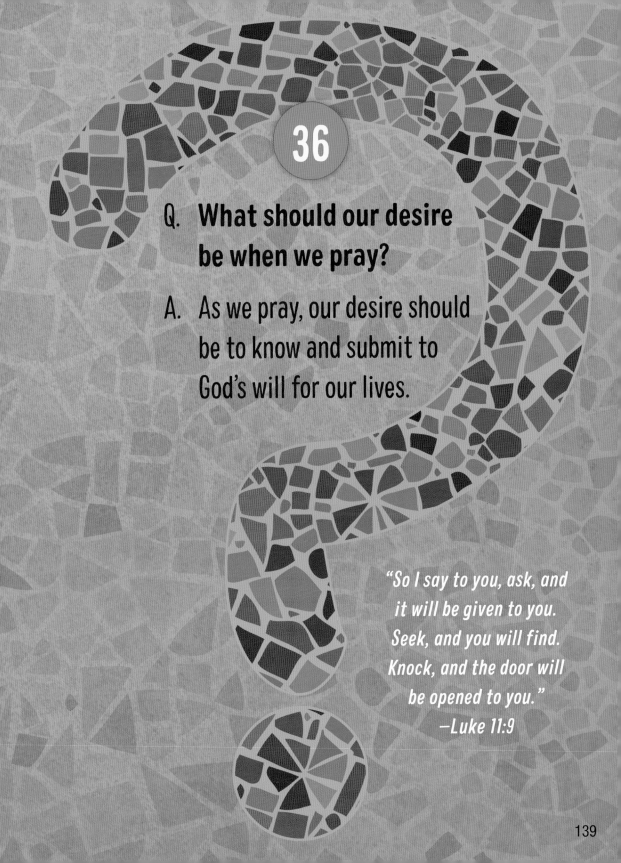

36

Q. **What should our desire be when we pray?**

A. As we pray, our desire should be to know and submit to God's will for our lives.

"So I say to you, ask, and it will be given to you. Seek, and you will find. Knock, and the door will be opened to you."
—Luke 11:9

37

Q. What should our attitude be
as we submit to God's will?

A. We should submit to
God's will with joy.

*Rejoice in the Lord always.
I will say it again: Rejoice!*
—Philippians 4:4

38

Q. What is worship?

A. *Worship* is declaring and celebrating
the great worth of God.

39

Q. When should we worship God?

A. We should worship God at all times in all we do.

40

Q. How do we worship God?

A. We worship God by ourselves and with other believers as part of a church.

Come, let us worship and bow down;
let us kneel before the Lord our Maker.
For he is our God, and we are the people of
his pasture, the sheep under his care.
—Psalm 95:6-7

The CHURCH and Last Things

And he subjected everything under his feet and appointed him as head over everything for the church, which is his body, the fullness of the one who fills all things in every way.
—Ephesians 1:22–23

1

Q. **What is the church?**

A. The *church* is a local community of Christians who are committed to one another and gather together regularly.

2

Q. **When did the church begin?**

A. The church began at Pentecost, shortly after Jesus ascended into heaven.

When the day of Pentecost had arrived, they were all together in one place. Suddenly a sound like that of a violent rushing wind came from heaven, and it filled the whole house where they were staying.
—Acts 2:1-2

3

Q. **Who is head of the church?**

A. Jesus is the head, or leader, of the church.

4

Q. **What leaders has Jesus given the church under Him?**

A. Jesus has given pastors, elders, and deacons to lead the church under Him.

5

Q. **Why does the church exist?**

A. The church exists to glorify God by worshiping together, growing together, and taking the gospel to all the world.

6

Q.   **What unites a church?**

A.   The gospel of Jesus Christ
     unites a church.

*They devoted themselves to the apostles' teaching, to
the fellowship, to the breaking of bread, and to prayer.*
—Acts 2:42

7

Q. **What is the gospel?**

A. The *gospel* is the good news of how God has provided forgiveness of sin through Jesus and how Jesus will restore all things one day.

For I passed on to you as most important what I also received: that Christ died for our sins according to the Scriptures, that he was buried, that he was raised on the third day according to the Scriptures.
—1 Corinthians 15:3-4

8

Q. **What two ordinances has Jesus given the church?**

A. Jesus has given the church the ordinances of baptism and the Lord's Supper.

9

Q. **Why did Jesus give these two ordinances?**

A. Jesus gave these two ordinances to help us remember what He has done and that we belong to Him.

"I pray not only for these, but also for those who believe in me through their word. May they all be one, as you, Father, are in me and I am in you. May they also be in us, so that the world may believe you sent me."
—John 17:20-21

10

Q. What is the Lord's Supper?

A. The *Lord's Supper* is eating the bread and drinking of the cup to remember the life, death, and resurrection of Jesus as we also look forward to His coming kingdom.

11

Q. What does the bread represent?

A. The bread represents the body of Jesus that was broken on the cross.

For as often as you eat this bread and drink the cup, you proclaim the Lord's death until he comes.
—1 Corinthians 11:26

12

Q. What does the cup represent?

A. The cup represents the blood of Jesus that was shed on the cross for the forgiveness of sin.

13

Q. **What is baptism?**

A. *Baptism* is a symbol of how God has given us new life in Christ and joined us with Him and the church.

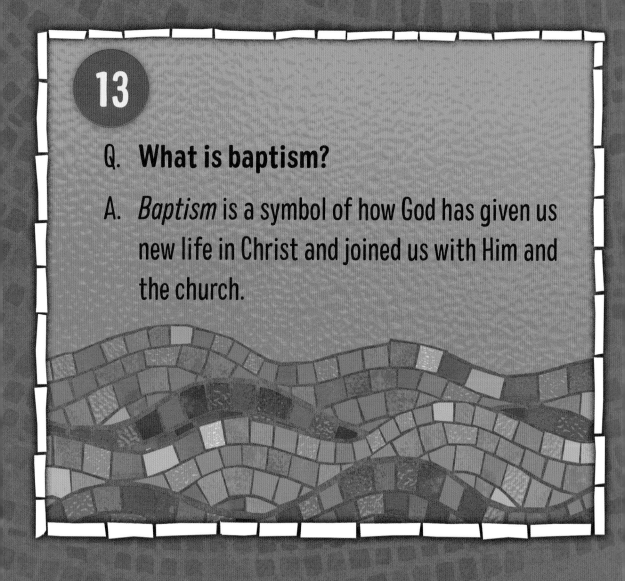

14

Q. **What is the hope of the church?**

A. The hope of the church is the return of Jesus when He will make all things new.

15

Q. **When will Jesus return?**

A. Jesus will return in God's perfect timing.

"If I go away and prepare a place for you, I will come again and take you to myself, so that where I am you may be also."
—John 14:3

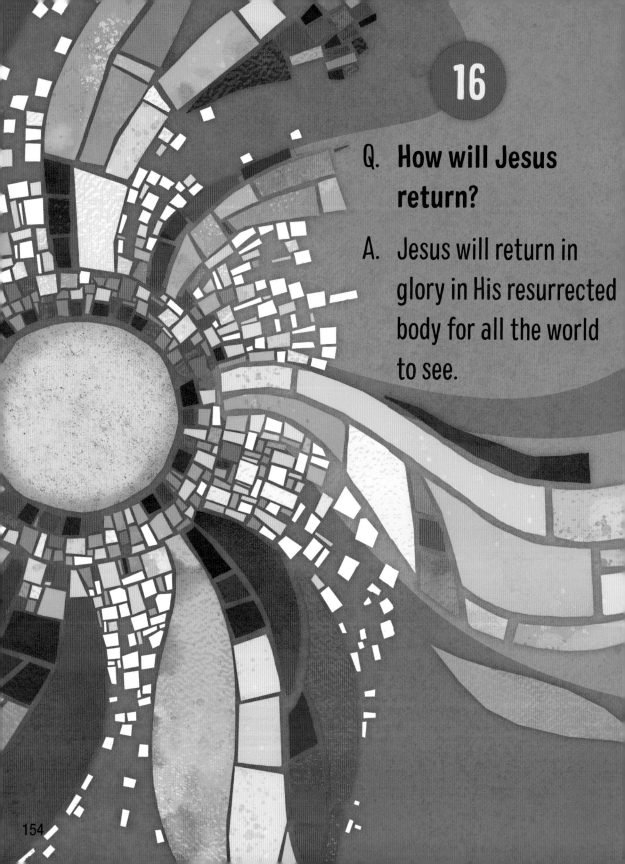

16

Q. **How will Jesus return?**

A. Jesus will return in glory in His resurrected body for all the world to see.

17

Q. When Jesus returns, what will happen to all the people who have died?

A. All the dead will be raised again when Jesus returns.

18

Q. What will happen to everyone who has not believed in Jesus when He returns?

A. Everyone who has not believed in Jesus will be judged for his or her sins and be separated from God forever.

Look, he is coming with the clouds, and every eye will see him, even those who pierced him. And all the tribes of the earth will mourn over him. So it is to be. Amen.
—Revelation 1:7

19

Q. **What will happen to everyone who has believed in Jesus when He returns?**

A. Everyone who has believed in Jesus will be rewarded for his or her faithfulness and be with God forevermore.

20

Q. **What will happen to the world when Jesus returns?**

A. When Jesus returns, the world will be made right once again and God's kingdom will come in fullness.

Then I heard a loud voice from the throne: Look, God's dwelling is with humanity, and he will live with them. They will be his peoples, and God himself will be with them and will be their God. He will wipe away every tear from their eyes. Death will be no more; grief, crying, and pain will be no more, because the previous things have passed away.

—Revelation 21:3-4

Remember

"Therefore, everyone who hears these words of mine and acts on them will be like a wise man who built his house on the rock."—Matthew 7:24

Read

Read Matthew 7:24–27. The Bible is one big story telling us about who God is, how we can know Him through Jesus, and how we can live for Him. When we trust in Jesus, God changes our hearts. We want to live for God because we love Him and are grateful for what He has done for us.

We can't miss that last point! It's what Jesus was talking about in Matthew 7 at the end of the Sermon on the Mount. Hearing God's truth isn't enough. Hearing and believing God's truth isn't enough either. Jesus told us that we are to hear, believe, and live God's truth. Everything we do in life—school, sports, hobbies, how we spend our money and time—is to be done for God.

It all begins with knowing God and loving Him. If we don't know God, it's hard to know how to live for Him. And if we don't love God, it's hard to want to live for Him. Know God. Love God. That's a solid foundation to build on!

Think

1. Why do you think some people do not live the way they know God wants them to live? Is following God difficult for you sometimes too? Why?

2. Jesus said the Bible is like a strong foundation to stand on. How can the Bible help us when life is difficult, such as when someone is being unkind to us, when we feel lonely, or when we are tempted to sin?

3. What are some reasons you can love God? Hint: Think about who He is, what He has done, and what He has promised.

4. What have you learned about God from this book? What are some things you don't know about Him but wish you did? Have you tried looking in the Bible to find out?

5. Which questions and answers in this book were the hardest for you to memorize or understand? What helped you to memorize questions and answers in the book? How might that help you memorize Bible verses too?

6. How would you describe what the Bible is about to a friend who doesn't know what it is?

7. What is one way you can show God's love to someone else this week? Whom can you tell about Jesus?

A PARENT'S GUIDE TO *CORNERSTONES:*

200 QUESTIONS AND ANSWERS TO LEARN TRUTH

This Parent Guide provides parents with two hundred questions and answers about God the Father, God the Son, God the Holy Spirit, sin, redemption, the church, discipleship, and more. Each question and answer is written to make these foundational truths accessible for a child. Additional commentary is provided to equip parents to engage in meaningful conversations about God in everyday life.

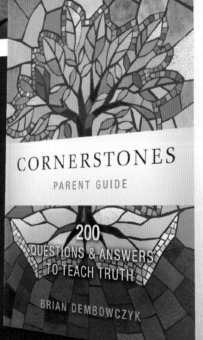

CORNERSTONES

PARENT GUIDE

200 QUESTIONS & ANSWERS TO TEACH TRUTH

BRIAN DEMBOWCZYK

Available wherever books are sold.